Manifesting The Life You Desire

Teri Van Horn

Copyright © 2012 Teri Van Horn

All rights reserved.

ISBN-10: 1479175986
ISBN-13: 978-1479175987

Other Titles by Teri Van Horn

365 Days of Blessings

Harness the Power of the Light

The Magic of Crystals

The Mystery of Crystals

The Crystal Healers

Copyright 2012 – 2015 Teri Van Horn
All Rights Reserved
Unauthorized duplication is a violation of applicable US and International laws.

No part of this book may be reproduced in any manner or otherwise copied for public or private use – except in the case of brief quotations embodied in critical reviews and articles – without prior written permission of the author and publisher.

The author of this book does not dispense medical advice or prescribe the use of any technique as a form of treatment for physical, emotional or medical problems without the advice of a physician, either directly or indirectly. The intent of the author is only to offer information of a general nature to help the reader in their quest for emotional and spiritual well-being. The author assumes no responsibility for the reader's actions.

Teri Van Horn

DEDICATION

We all have special people in our lives, who bring out the best in us. Mine just happened to be my father, Ray Mathews. Daddy was a one-in-a-million… a wonderful father, loyal husband and the best friend anyone could ask for.

He thought about things that other people just didn't.
One evening, after my daughter had been born and everyone was busy with the baby, he leaned over to me and said, "We love her very much, but don't forget we'll always love you first." I can't tell you how much that meant to a young, overwhelmed and exhausted mother!

That's the way he was, he didn't say a lot, but when he spoke, it was meaningful. He's been gone for many years now, but is always in my heart and close to my thoughts.

If it hadn't been for his unconditional love and encouragement, I don't know where I'd be today.

CONTENTS

	Introduction	i
1	Manifesting Your Ideal Life	1
2	Follow Your Bliss	4
3	Discovering Your Purpose	12
4	Finding What You Do Best	19
5	Rediscovering Who You Really Are	23
6	Focusing On Your Potential	27
7	Set Yourself Apart	33
8	Your Belief System	37
9	Roadblocks To Success	41
10	Reality Check	45
11	Change Your Thoughts – Change Your Life	50
12	Laws of Attraction & Affirmations	54
13	Universal Laws	63
14	Attitude of Gratitude	75
15	Vision Boards – Using Your Senses	80
16	Powerful Prayers	87
17	Putting It All Together	95

INTRODUCTION

Twenty-five years ago, I saw my first passion vine. I was enthralled with its exotic beauty, while appreciating its delicacy. I immediately went to the local hardware store to purchase lattice for it to climb, potting soil to live in and the largest pot of passion vine that I could afford. I worked and worked to create the special flowerbed for this beautiful vine, but it eventually succumbed to life in suburbia. I couldn't save it, but I always remembered how it made me feel and how much I enjoyed watching the butterflies enjoy its nectar.

A lot of things have changed in those twenty-five years, but the dreams I had never did. I took several wrong turns (as we all do), but I always kept the goals in my sights, always working towards reaching them, in whatever manner I could at the time. Believe me, it wasn't all easy, but I did it!

It took me a while, but I finally learned how to make my dreams come true and how to manifest what I wanted for my life.

Today, I live on a small ranch in the Texas Hill Country, with a loving and very supportive husband. I have a gorgeous and brilliant daughter, with an equally handsome and brilliant son-in-law. Both of whom I am very proud.

Together, we have nine horses – two of which are babies, and four dogs who sleep in the driveway in a feeble effort to keep us safe. I have wonderful and supportive friends, a job where I'm able to go out and help people, and…

a pasture *FULL* of passion vines!

You can manifest the life you desire, I'm living proof!

Blessings,

Teri

Manifesting The Life You Desire

The Lotus has always been the emblem of the spiritual aspirant.
It rises from its origins in the mud of material life,
through the often murky waters of thoughts and emotions
to open its pure, fragrant, golden heart to the sun.
While remaining firmly rooted in the mud, it floats serenely unaffected on the surface of the water,
basking in the Light and inspiring all with its sweet fragrance and natural beauty.

Namasté ॐ

1

MANIFESTING YOUR IDEAL LIFE

Everywhere you look it seems people are talking, writing or teaching about manifestation, visualization, and the laws of attraction. There have been books about The Secret, The Prayer of Jabez, Creative Visualization and hundreds of others over the years and I think I've read almost every one of them. Everyone wants success – everyone wants prosperity – everyone wants everything… NOW!

How do we achieve this? There are many, many ways to achieve success – just as there are many definitions of success.

Success to some is material wealth, for others it might be peace of mind, a sense of security, good health, achieving your dreams, happy relationships – the list could go on and on as there are as many definitions as there are people!

The key to Manifesting the Life You Desire is to first define what your desires are. Go inside and think about what you really want and desire. Knowing what you truly want in life is the most important aspect of manifestation.

They say that knowledge is power… and in this case knowledge is everything!

So that's where we begin, getting to know what YOU really believe, want and desire. This is a process – it can't happen in a day. You can't rush through reading this to find your pot of gold. You must first decide what exactly is within that pot… it may be gold, it may be enlightenment, it may be simply being at peace with yourself.

This is a journey – and like all trips, you need a destination and a map to get there. If you've ever looked up travel directions on the internet, you've often found that there are various methods to get to where you desire. Some are direct, some are scenic, some take you all over the place and some get you there without passing "Go". It is up to you which method is best for you. That is why we offer several different methods for this internal journey – so that you can choose what works best for you. Any of these methods can and will be successful, if you apply them faithfully.

It's certainly ok to try different methods. That's the beauty of this type of thing. Intent far outweighs perfection in theory! Take time to learn about what really brings focus and purpose into your life, and then build on it. Don't worry about changing your purpose – I've changed mine as I've grown and learned over the years. It's all just part of the process..

The more you know about the unknown, the more you actually understand how little you know. It makes you humble and brings you back to the world of wonders, miracles and magic,

A world in which everything is possible!

2

FOLLOW YOUR BLISS, THINKING IS BELIEVING

For years, this was *the* catchphrase… Follow Your Bliss. I remember hearing Marianne Williamson shout this to the rooftops… Follow Your Bliss, Follow Your Bliss! It's a great idea… assuming you know what your *Bliss* actually is.

We are constantly told what to think and feel by our friends, family, society, government and heritage. But what do YOU really think and feel?

What defines your Bliss… your happiness?

I'm sure you can list a hundred things, right off the bat, but will this be a lasting happiness or bliss, or is it just temporary? Like the proverbial genie who gives you three wishes... which ones will truly make you happy six months to a year from now?

Our society is based on instant gratification, 'me first', lack of responsibility and being environmentally destructive. Focusing on the 'greater good' is mostly a thing of the past. BUT... if we believe that everything is ruled by cause and effect, then we're in a world of trouble!

Our old concepts have led to a society that is self-centered, ego-driven, and irresponsible. We have become a bunch of happiness seekers who are only satisfied by buying more useless stuff on a daily basis so that we can create the illusion of perfection, happiness and completeness. This places us in a never-ending cycle of working someplace that doesn't fulfill our soul purpose in order to make more money so we can buy things that don't ultimately make us happy.

We immerse ourselves with outside distractions: TV, movies, books, the internet, social networking, sports, and a myriad of other things so that we might be entertained or happy for a few fleeting moments.

When I volunteer with children at our local elementary school, the children have such a hard time sitting still, listening or focusing. They're so accustomed to having things told to them through all the technical and electronic resources, that they have a hard time sitting down and making-up a story on their own. Many don't know how to think for themselves when they come upon a problem and are always asking someone else to tell them the answers. By being raised with all these distractions, from a very early age, they no longer have the ability to listen to that voice inside that has all the answers they'll ever need.

We're so busy chasing 'the dream' that we forget that true happiness lies within.

I see so many people these days who spend most of their time on their computers or in front of the TV, only to say that they're constantly bored or unhappy. Why? Because they have NO idea who they really are!

As children they are given electronic toys that do everything for them, which destroys their ability to think, create and use their imagination. The BEST gifts you can give a child are a stack of blank paper and a crayon. Let them create a fantasy world. Let them use their imagination and create silly drawings or stories. Allow them to dream! When you take away their ability to use their imagination, you're turning them into robots who now have to be constantly entertained and who are incapable of discovering and getting to know who they really are as a person.

If someone is continually watching the news, playing violent video games or watches TV or movies based in violence – they're going to believe that the world is a violent and negative place. That's where their thought process is going to focus.

We've all heard that we are what we think and it's true! Our thoughts create our reality! That's not to say that if we believe that there's a pink and yellow dragon sitting in the dining room that one will be there next time we walk by – but if we believe something and repeat those thoughts over and over, we can turn that into our reality.

That's not to say that we can sit at home and 'believe' that money is going to come raining down upon us at any moment and it'll happen. We have to use our thoughts and belief system along with being proactive to achieve our greatest dreams and desires.

What is your thought process?

William James said it best, "The greatest discovery of my generation is that human beings can alter their lives by altering their attitudes of mind."

Think about the life you are currently living. Are you living your dream? Do you have the home you've wanted? What about your lifestyle – is it what you've desired? How about your job – is it what you imagined as a small child? Everything that you are experiencing today is a product of manifestation… whether it's good or bad… it's what you've created.

How did you create this? By your thought process! Everything that you are experiencing is a product of your thought process. Your thoughts have created the framework for your reality. Everything you think, say or do ends up creating your reality!

Come on, how can this be possible, you might ask. The answer can come in two ways – but ends up being the same result – everything is energy.

If you study physics, they will tell you that everything is comprised of energy from molecules. If you want to think of this from a spiritual level, everything comes from the Source/God and is energy.

Yes, Everything is Energy!

You might not be able to see it, but everything has a vibrational frequency to go along with those molecules. Therefore for every action there is a reaction in the universe… and that applies in our own lives as well.

For example – We've all met someone who's always in a bad mood, someone who lives an "Eyore" existence. Think about their life – is it happy or is everything gloomy?

What about the person who is always positive and in a great mood? What is their life like? Do things seem to go easier for them? Are they more successful or have more friends?

Of course you can argue that each of these people's attitudes are determined by their lifestyle – not the other way around. BUT… I believe and have seen many, many times that we all create our lifestyles through our attitudes.

As children we are all labeled by others. Some are considered the 'pretty ones', some are the 'smart ones', some are the 'quiet ones' and others the 'wild ones'. How did these labels affect you as a child? Did they help create your reality as you were growing up? How have they helped you manifest or create the life you're living today?

Everything starts with an idea or thought, which is energy, which creates vibrations that we send out to the world. Your thoughts are nothing more than vibrations that resonate with similar vibrations that already exist. If you don't believe this, here's an experiment for you… take two stringed instruments and place them side by side. Pluck the string of one and you will notice that the string on the other will begin vibrating. That is the principal of resonance and it applies as much to your thoughts as it does those strings!

Your thoughts create your reality, it's just that simple. If you control your thoughts, you'll be able to control, create and manifest your reality. If your mind is going in a hundred different directions, your life will be just as unfocused. Also, if you are unable to control your thoughts and your mind is in constant chaos, things will manifest that are random and unconnected, because they will have been manifested by other people for you.

You've heard the saying, "Your outer world is a reflection of your inner world!" That one hits home! If your world is chaotic or negative, it's a very good assumption that your inner world – your thoughts – are the same.

Our minds are like radios. We send out our thoughts, feelings and energy – and we are able to pick-up on these from others, as well. Some people are very attuned to this and we refer to them as psychics. Most of us have walked into a room before and 'felt' the emotion in it, whether it was good or bad. We receive as well as send out energy and vibrations.

Sometimes we send and sometimes we receive… the trick is to find the balance and learn when to create things and when to sit back and receive the experiences.

In each and every moment we are able to make a conscious decision about what we want to send and to receive into our lives. It can be positive or negative… it's all up to you!

We have several thousand thoughts in a given day. Sit down and think about what you *think* about. Are you positive or negative? Do you think about lack or prosperity? As Randy Pausch used to ask, are you a Tigger or an Eyore? How do your thoughts correspond to the life you're living?

3

DISCOVERING YOUR PURPOSE

Stated simply, there are two basic energies in the world: love and fear. High vibrations stem from love/being positive and low vibrations stem from fear/being negative. The high, loving vibrations are directly related to being on the path to fulfilling your true purpose in life.

Each of us is here for a reason, to realize the soul's true purpose. Though a soulful focus may sound esoteric, it is actually simple and at the same time, very important.

The soul's calling can be found in your greatest joy and excitement. Key points to remember:

When you pursue the inner joy and excitement of the soul, you feel loving, open, and alive. You are following your true calling. You feel happy and energized by the high vibrations you are generating. Love allows you to feel good about yourself and seek inner fulfillment. You are a free spirit who can step out of the crowd to follow your own path and create an extraordinary life.

When you ignore the calling of the soul, you feel fearful, stuck, and depressed. You are following the limited perspective of the wounded ego and your soul's calling is repressed by the low vibrations you are generating. You feel unsure of yourself and seek others' approval as a way to feel better. Fear prevents you from trying something different, so you follow the norm, and lead an ordinary life.

With this in mind, it makes sense to set a course that aligns you with your soul's greatest joys and the highest vibrations you can muster. In his book *A New Earth*, Eckhart Tolle describes joy as the sense of aliveness that emerges when the creative power of the universe becomes conscious of itself. "Through enjoyment, you link into that universal creative power itself." The phenomenon of suffering and waiting for a better time or whatever the excuse is to follow our true joy and excitement is a trap we fall into when we are not consciously in command of our lives.

Wherever you are now, you can open to the infinite. You have the opportunity today, right this minute, to set your course and create an extraordinarily magical and joyful life.

Of course all of this sounds simple and great in theory and for some people knowing what they want might not be that easy. We have to break out from what we've been told or conditioned. We need to do the hard work… turn off the TV, put down the computer and look within. I mean REALLY look within! For some people, they already have the answers, for others it may take months, weeks or even years to discover their purpose or what they truly want from life.

A good way to get started is to take pen to paper and answer the following questions:

The trick here is to take logic, fear and doubt (i.e. the ego) out of the equation and just think outside of the box.

- ~ What is my deepest desire?
- ~ What would I like to accomplish in my life?
- ~ What am I good at?
- ~ What makes me feel complete?
- ~ What resonates within me?
- ~ Is there something I feel particularly drawn to?

When asking yourself these questions, think about all areas of your life:

- Work
- Relationships
- Health
- Finances
- How you spend your free time

Once you begin to start defining what your goals might be, don't stop there. Keep going! Get into specifics. For example if you've decided that teaching is something you feel strongly about, don't stop there. Think about:

- Do I want to teach adults, children or those with special needs?
- What subjects or skills do I want to teach?
- Do I want to teach through an institution, tutor or start my own practice?
- What credentials do I have in order to teach?
- What credentials do I need so I can teach?
- How can I go about teaching?
- Does this feel like the most right thing in the world for me?

That last question is key... is this the most right thing for YOU? Not your family, not your friends, not your job... does this feel right to you?

Do this exercise for each of your goals. After you have written each of them down, set priorities making the most important one first and going on down the list. Now that you have these prioritized, you now know where you can start focusing your thoughts and energies. By doing this exercise, you are programming your consciousness to spend time according to what's most important on your list.

Of course simply making the list and putting it in order isn't all you'll have to do to start manifesting your dreams. You'll have to put some effort into this project, as well. In the movie "The Music Man" Professor Henry Hill promises the boys who join the band will be successful by using the 'Think Method' in spite of not having instruments. I'm here to tell you that the 'Think Method' is only part of the equation... you really need those instruments, too!

That being said, you can't sit on the sofa all day and keep telling yourself that you're going to be a great teacher (or whatever your goal may be). You're going to have to take steps toward making this goal and dream come alive, for example:

~ Start researching to see what is needed to become the type of teacher you want to be.

- Book a seminar on a subject that intrigues you.
- Attend workshops in your area of interest.
- Start networking with others about this subject.
- Find out if there are opportunities for you to volunteer your services while gaining experience in this particular field.

The more time you focus you energy towards this goal, the greater the chances are that you will succeed and accomplish the goal. Five minutes a day isn't going to take you very far – you'll need to put some honest and sincere effort towards being successful.

Another very important aspect of manifestation is consistency. Once you've created you list of goals and prioritized them, you'll need to make certain that this feels good emotionally, as well. Everything must feel right and of value to you. Otherwise you'll have a very hard time devoting time, energy and effort towards them.

Achieving goals often takes time and this is something that stops many people in their tracks. After the initial excitement of getting started, you have to stay focused in making your goals a reality. Oftentimes people don't see results as quickly as they'd like and they get discouraged, thinking that their goal isn't achievable. OR insecurity and self-doubt start jumping in making them think that their goal wasn't meant for them or that they'll never be able to accomplish what they set out to do.

This is where you need to assess where these feelings are coming from. Is this pressure from outside sources? Are you really doubting yourself or are you just being impatient? You need to acknowledge where these thoughts and feelings are coming from and deal with them. Simply ignoring these negative thoughts isn't going to stop them. Understandably you're discouraged because you assume that things should be happening sooner, when often times, you're just not ready.

There are no unrealistic goals – only unrealistic time frames!

Remember those road maps… not every path is direct, some may take you the scenic route and although that might take a little longer, the view is often worth it.

When we try too hard, we start forcing things and increasing pressure on ourselves. That doesn't do anyone any good – in fact, it'll start pushing our goal away from us. Relax, take a deep cleansing breath and continue moving along with the belief that there is nothing you can't accomplish.

What to do when you feel "stuck"?

4

FINDING WHAT YOU DO BEST

Everyone has special gifts and talents, no matter who they are. This is something that is within each of us, a combination of energy patterns that direct us towards certain things or ways of being. One of your most important tasks in this life is finding these special gifts and talents within yourself. This is a great way of celebrating who you truly are!

The secret to most successful people is that they have tapped into those special gifts and love what they do. How could you possibly be successful hating what you do? Find, and then follow that bliss!

Recognizing your special gifts and talents is essential for progressing in life and for manifesting the life you desire. Write down your gifts and talents so that they'll not only become more real to you, but that you'll be able to see how they can help in manifesting your goals.

Following are some questions to ask in order to create this list. Don't try to think about this too hard – these answers should come easily to you:

Think about your childhood:

- ~ What toys did you like to play with?
- ~ What were you interested in?
- ~ What imaginary games did you enjoy playing?
- ~ What did you dream about doing when you grew up?

Ask you closest friends to be 100% honest with you and ask them to take a fresh look at you when they give you an honest opinion about:

- ~ What do they think you're good at?
- ~ What do they think your talents are?
- ~ What do they think you should do with your life?

Now ask yourself a few questions. After getting information from these sources, keep an open mind and ask yourself a few questions. Don't take them too seriously, write down the first thing you think of. Allow these questions to expand your consciousness and think outside of the box. Your mind is part of the collective consciousness;

therefore you have access to all information. Your mind is connected to the infinite source of all existence, so relax and let it open freely while you answer these questions:

- What would you do if you never had to work again?
- What were your dreams when you were younger?
- What do you think is impossible for you to do?
- What would you do if this were the last day of your life?
- What would you do if you knew you only had one year to live?
- What would you do if you knew you couldn't fail?
- What are your strengths and talents?
- Do you have a wish but don't know how to fulfill it?
- What do you admire most about others?
- What would your idea lifestyle look like?
- What does success mean to you?
- What really makes you happy?
- What would be a perfect day for you?
- What would you do if there were no restrictions?
- What really excites you?
- What would you like to be honored and recognized for?
- Where do you see your life in ten years?
- If you were immortal, what would you do with your life?
- What needs to change to make this a better world?

- ~ What would you do if you could do anything?
- ~ What are you most proud of?
- ~ What would you like to accomplish this year?
- ~ What would you do differently if you could start over again?
- ~ Given the time, money and opportunity – what would you most like to accomplish?

Finding your special gifts and talents will provide you with your unique potential. This is the unique gift that came with you when you were born – the gift that you are asked to nourish in order to use it to guide your own life.

Don't let someone else's ideas or dreams replace that of your own. Chase your own dreams, follow your own destiny and achieve your own goals. That is what you came here to do.

If you don't discover your special gifts and talents, and are able to utilize them, you'll always have a void in your life. Find a way to dig deeper into yourself. Spend 30 minutes of 'me time' daily just to listen. Peel off the layers so that you can discover who you truly are and what you're meant to do in this life. This process can take time, energy and effort – but it's your life and you are certainly more than worth it! Getting to know your gifts and talents should be your top priority so that you can start to work manifesting your dreams and goals.

5

RE-DISCOVERING WHO YOU REALLY ARE

By now you should have a pretty good idea of what your particular gifts and talents are. You are truly gifted and unique! Are you gifted in dealing with those who have special needs, can you teach, do you like working with animals or children? Maybe your talents lie in organization or different aspects of business, design, or computer programming. Should you sing, dance or act? There are millions of things out there that are available – it's up to you to choose your own path!

This knowledge should give you confidence and a sense of stability… you now have some idea of what you brought into this lifetime and what you are here for.

Make a commitment to follow these gifts and talents; let them guide you and don't let anyone tell you what you should be doing. Never allow anyone to tell you that you're not good enough to fulfill your dreams. Identify and focus on your dreams as much as possible, as they are the surest guides in your life and will show you where to go. Remember that these are YOUR dreams… not someone else's, so don't let anyone discourage your progress.

This is YOUR path!!!

That being said, not all paths are easy. Now that you've gone through the process, you may discover that following your dreams is difficult. You may find yourself alone in the world, people may not understand and pull away. Some even might think you're crazy if your dreams don't match what they think you should be doing. Don't bow into pressure!

Remember… this is your path… this is your ultimate potential… no one else's.

Sometimes following your path can be difficult, but given enough time to develop your special gifts and talents, the stronger they will grow inside you, until they become your life force. They might start out as weaknesses, but they'll end up as strengths as you manifest your dreams.

Not everyone gets to have the prettiest or most glamorous gifts. Just know that the gifts and talents you have are yours alone and that they serve a purpose. We may not know why or how, but each of us has come to earth to experience life fully, regardless of our purpose.

What's the point – particularly if it's not a 'pretty' purpose? (for example: migrant farm workers – that's not a 'pretty' lifestyle, but still very important on many levels) Knowing your purpose, even if it involves a negative experience at a certain level, will free you from becoming a victim. You will have the understanding that you choose this experience and even the most negative things result in beautiful revelations and lessons. You can grow with the experience, achieving the lesson and wisdom you needed to learn. There are no mistakes in life – only opportunities – so we need to make the most of them, regardless of where life takes us. We all need to keep in mind that we are all important, we just have different jobs to do.

We all have a different path and understanding this will help release any thoughts of jealousy or resentment of those who might have more. As we said before, all paths are different, some are direct, some are scenic. We all take the path that is right for us that the time and need to understand that we are doing exactly the right thing, regardless of what it may be. Being on your own unique path is where you belong; it is the only way to achieve your dreams and Manifest the life you desire.

The soul is where our dreams and visions are born. It understands our mission (our life purpose) and it is this purpose that drives everything else.

6

FOCUSING ON YOUR POTENTIAL

Our ability to focus and turn our attention inward is one of our most important gifts. Thankfully, it is one we have all been given – whether we choose to use it or not. The word attention means "to turn one's mind towards" – to turn one's mind or senses; the act of applying the mind to an object of sense or thought.

It is the act of taking possession by the mind of one of several simultaneously possible objects or trains of thought. It implies withdrawal from some things in order to deal effectively with others.

What a wonderful gift! Our ability to focus our attention assists us in many ways, including our perception of reality. What we pay attention to or focus on is our reality. Other things, we ignore and they fade in significance for us, regardless of how important they may actually be.

We are able to choose what we focus on, our gifts, talents, home, community, friends, family, this choice is mostly unconscious and just happens. We rarely can recount everything we've encountered or experienced, but are able to remember what we've been paying attention to most over the years. This applies to our impressions of people, our world and ourselves. Someone once said that reality is 95% perception. It's what we pay attention to that makes our reality – it's not always what our reality actually 'is'.

The key to creating and manifesting our dreams and reality is based on what we focus on. Mastering and controlling our attention gives us the freedom to choose what happens in our lives.

We can choose to focus on the outside world, allowing it to influence our thoughts and actions – or we can focus within and listen to our truest self.

There are millions of things happening at the same time all over the world, but the only thing that is real to us is what we are focusing on. None of the other things are real to us, regardless of what they may be.

Control your focus. The more you can control your attention the more you are able to attract only the things in your life that you really want. If you don't pay attention to the negative things in your life, you will not create that reality.

This doesn't mean that you should go around with a Pollyanna approach to life, but you shouldn't get absorbed in the negative areas of life. Bless it, release it and move on to focusing on the important goals and dreams in your life.

A great analogy for attention is the faucet in your garden. You open it and see an endless stream of water flowing. Now you connect to it a hose, and with this hose you are able to direct the flow of water anywhere you decide. You may decide to water your rosebush in the back. You take the hose and direct it toward the rosebush and water it. Now, what happens when your hose has holes and leaks?

Let's assume for this analogy that your hose is really old and that there are many holes and leaks. The water is our analogy for the free attention you have in life. Taking a close look at the hose reveals that it is leaking in several places, and that the water is missing your rosebush entirely but plenty is flowing down into the earth to nourish the weeds that are dormant and only need a good drink to begin to sprout. If you look at the end of the hose you will notice there is not much water left for the rosebush.

Two things are happening here:

1. Your attention goes somewhere you would rather not have it go and things are happening that you *don't want* to have happen.

2. Your attention is not focused enough to have an effect on what you *do want* to accomplish.

It's very important that you learn to focus your attention. No one wants a 'monkey mind' jumping around from branch to branch, tree to tree, never stopping, always swinging around getting into mischief and wreaking havoc. (which is exactly what happens when the 'monkey mind' is given control) One very simple way to focus your attention is to say your thoughts aloud as they come into your head. It's best to do this when you're alone so no one thinks you're crazy! It's a great way to see just how scattered you really are.

Some thoughts might be:

- ~ What I'll be doing tomorrow…
- ~ What I need to do today…
- ~ What errands I need to run…
- ~ Oh – I forgot to do laundry!
- ~ I need to have the car washed…

- The dog needs to go to the vet…
- I need to stop by the cleaners….
- We're out of milk! I have to run by the store…
- When is this monkey mind going to stop?
- I need some 'me time'.
- What's for dinner…
- I'm exhausted!
- I'll never get these things done.
- My boss hates me…

The list never ends! But at least you'll be consciously aware of what you are thinking and how you are literally programming yourself minute by minute. As quickly as these thoughts race through our mind, it's no wonder why we're so stressed, physically ill, overwhelmed and can never seem to reach our goals. When could we possibly have time with all of these thoughts running through our heads?

Take time every day to focus on your thoughts. What are you saying to yourself? Do you now see how you've been programming your life with this constantly litany of things? Take time to spend at least 15 minutes each day focusing on these thoughts and you will start to see several changes. Your mind will start becoming calmer. Of course, you may still feel exhausted and it'll probably be difficult to stop in the beginning, but don't give up. Training your mind not to exhaust itself will sharpen your focus and free- up your attention considerably. The more free attention you have, the happier you'll feel and the more power you have to control what is happening in your life.

Try to stay away from things that waste our time, destroy our focus and redirect our attention. You know what they are… TV, advertising, the internet, computer games, magazines, whiners & complainers, large crowds, loud noises, junk mail, newspapers, the news. All of these can break our focus and prevent us from listening within. Advertising is the biggest culprit because they're always telling us how we need to improve our lives, home, family, ourselves… we need to deliberately choose to not give our attention away to these companies and focus it on ourselves.

You have infinite attention.

It's up to you as to how you choose to focus it!

Practice quieting your mind so that you can then learn to re-direct it's attention on the things you desire the most.

By looking inward, you'll discover everything you need.

7

SET YOURSELF APART

By now you've decided what your goals, special gifts and talents are. You've also discovered that you're harboring a 'monkey mind' that needs to be released. So how do you go from here to manifesting the life you desire?

This is where our road begins to branch off and everyone is able to start experimenting with the path that best suits them. Before we reach the fork in the road, there are still a couple more processes we need to work through.

The first is exploring the world of virtual reality… your imagination!

__Your mind and imagination are such amazing gifts.__

You can visualize things you've never seen before, you can close your eyes and 'see' things that you have seen before. You can visit great mystical worlds or practice for an exam. Your mind doesn't have to obey the laws of gravity or physics – it just has to be creative.

Once you think of these things, they become a part of you and your memory. This ultimate playground is yours for the asking and you can do whatever you wish. You are also able to use your mind and imagination to help memorize things that you might be able to learn verbatim.

By using your imagination, you are able to expand your brain capacity and ability to store information. You are able to use the right and left hemisphere's together, which allows you to store information in your long-term memory. From there, the information is accessible at any time, even after many years have passed. If you only use one side of your brain, the information takes a longer time to get to your long-term memory – usually only effectively by repeating a task. Most of the time information gets stored in your short-term memory and is no longer available after a day or so. Isn't the mind a marvelous machine?

There are only three methods to store information in your long-term memory:

1. Repetition
2. Intensity
3. Using both sides of the brain simultaneously

So how does your imagination help with manifesting?

If you can imagine it, it won't be difficult to create it! Let's assume you want $20,000 in your bank account by the end of this month. Start using your imagination:

- ~ Visualize your bank statement reading your balance is $20,000
- ~ Visualize making a withdrawal and you are holding $20,000 in your hand
- ~ Visualize how you feel
- ~ Visualize bringing the money home and spreading it all over your table
- ~ Visualize what you can buy with this money

By doing this process you are already training your mind for the event of claiming $20,000. Your mind will start bringing up other pictures and stories when you do this exercise, for example:

- ~ A thought comes up... How bogus is this?
- ~ A thought comes up... I don't believe this will ever happen!
- ~ A thought comes up... Why not go for $50,000 or $100,000?
- ~ A feeling arises... you feel excited

- A picture arises… you only see $850 in your bank account
- A picture arises… you cannot see a number on your bank statement

These are all uncertainties of the mind that will vanish when you do the exercise several times. Do it often, until you are able to see exactly what you desire is happening. Do it until there is no other thought, feeling or picture coming up with that is not aligned with your goal.

You can also introduce your other senses into this practice. When doing your visualizations, say it aloud and write the story down. The more senses you involved in the process, the deeper the memory will become carved into your brain and the sooner it will become a reality.

Do this a couple times a day for a month and just see what happens… it may just surprise you!

8

YOUR BELIEF SYSTEM

Beliefs are concepts that we either come-up with on our own or take over from someone else. The ability to believe something is another great function of our minds. Beliefs are a built-in function of our consciousness and one of the most powerful instruments to shape our reality. It is so powerful, that when formulated from many people, can shift mass consciousness and lead to profound changes in our society. It even has the power to shift the collective consciousness of the whole of civilization.

The purpose of a belief is to make an experience, meaning, a belief is basically a concept, something that you assume, but actually don't know as a concrete fact. You only know something for sure when you have experienced it – everything else are concepts that we consider to comprise the basis of our knowledge. Our whole life is built around beliefs.

How we form our beliefs

There are two different ways you can live your life. The first way is to observe nature and then construct a belief around it. This is still currently the way we receive information in school; it is the way most people operate their lives. The problem with this approach is that it leads to a form of living that convinces us that we are not responsible for anything that happens in our lives. This approach leads to the idea that we cannot change things in our lives.

The second way is the opposite – you decide what you want to believe and later find the evidence of this belief in nature. Does this sound strange to you? Maybe not, maybe you already have shifted your consciousness into this new way of thinking.

What are the benefits of thinking this way?

You are responsible for what is happening in your life. You could also say that you have created it one way or another. Either you are conscious of being your life's creator or you are not. A lot of what we actually create happens unconsciously. Another benefit of thinking this way is that you can change what you'd like to experience by simply changing your beliefs and the concepts around them.

Understand how powerful this is! When you live your life as the master of your beliefs, you can handle anything because you ultimately know that you have created it. And even if you are not aware, you will at some point accept it.

By the act of believing, we form a unique structure in our consciousness, an energy pattern that acts like a blueprint for what we will experience in our life.

Reaction versus action

A reaction is an unconscious response to a given situation. Your consciousness is not involved and the outcome is random. Most of the time it is an answer that reflects what you have done in the past. It is a choice-less and powerless approach to handling a situation. An action is a deliberate choice you make. It is a response to a situation that is based on the result of consciously analyzing and contemplating a given situation. It empowers you and moves your life further along the path you have chosen.

Your action and the outcome of the situation are completely separate from and different from the idea of whether you believe something or not. Beliefs are very powerful. One way to determine what beliefs you want to take on is simply by looking for what the reality would be, that this belief would create. Is this belief supporting what I would like to experience or not?

Many of our beliefs are carried forward from our parents, from school, friends and news sources like radio and television. You have a choice to make about taking these beliefs on unfiltered, or by evaluating them and either accepting or rejecting them.

You will also experience that it is more important to understand *how you believe*, than *what your belief is.* Understanding the process of how you believe gives you tremendous power in your life. You will find that different sources of news are more or less credible to your beliefs. If your best friend tells you something you may believe it instantly, as you have known your friend for years and, in the past, your friend's information was always reliable. Getting information from strangers is a totally different story and the level of acceptance may be much lower. Most people willingly adopt the beliefs of their doctors completely as they may see them as the ultimate truth givers.

If you hold a belief that you 'know' to be true, you have given that belief the highest level of trustworthiness. However, understand that it is still a belief and not the truth. The truth as an absolute does not exist, even if you find all the evidence in the world for it, based on quantum physics theories.

9

ROADBLOCKS TO SUCCESS

At some point in everyone's life, we all ask the same questions: "Why are other people so successful, and I'm not?" Depending on how closely you look, you may find several reasons why this happens. Some familiar ones are:

- ~ They're just luckier than I am
- ~ They had a better education that I did
- ~ Their family is wealthy
- ~ They already had the money to start a business
- ~ They are smarter than I am
- ~ They are younger than I am
- ~ They're better looking than I am
- ~ They probably work harder than I do
- ~ Everything they touch turns to gold

- They married better than I did
- They have better connections that I do

This list could go on forever as money and wealth is the topic that generates the most beliefs.

You still may not realize it yet, but your beliefs are the blueprint for your reality.

If you knew that, would you deliberately create a thought for yourself from the list above? Probably not because these really aren't supported at all… these beliefs are more ranting that allows you to play the victim and keeps you exactly where you are. You're not improving your life with these excuses you're just saying things so that you'll feel better about yourself.

Why do we create these beliefs in the first place, knowing that they're not constructive? Most of us were told that there is a universe out there and that it shapes our reality. It is the basic belief that life happens to us – we have no control or responsibility over our destiny. The majority of us get these beliefs confirmed several times each day and the result is that our consciousness gets imprinted every day with the same message, with the same old erroneous belief.

As adults, we are not even aware that our life 'as it happens' is built around a belief. It becomes a reality that we prove to ourselves in each moment.

So how do we get out of this dilemma? We need to take a step back and look at our beliefs. Write down all the beliefs you have about money. Just be spontaneous and when you run out of your own beliefs, think about what other people's beliefs are about money.

When you've completed your list, next to each belief, mark it with B (for blocking wealth) or an S (for supporting wealth). Now look back over your list and count each blocking and supporting belief. What is your score? Do you have more blocking or supportive beliefs?

Realize that all the blocking beliefs do not support the creation of a fortune. Now, take a new piece of paper and brainstorm beliefs that will exactly create the wealth you would like to have. When you are done with the list, go over each of your new beliefs and create a mental image. Hold this mental image for at least 10-20 seconds. You may need some practice, but every time you do it, you'll get better. Do this exercise in a quiet, calm and relaxed environment, as this will help imprint these beliefs into your consciousness.

Beliefs are the blueprint of what you will manifest in your life.

With a little training, you'll be able to move onto the next state, which is feeling your beliefs. Feel as if these new beliefs, that support what you really want to create, have actually been manifested.

- ~ How does it feel to be a millionaire?
- ~ How does it feel to have abundance in your life?
- ~ How does it feel to have more money than you can spend?
- ~ How does it feel to give to others?
- ~ How does it feel to buy something without having to look at the price?

Whenever you catch yourself thinking or speaking about a blocking belief about money, stop what you are doing! Go back to the place in your mind where you recall one of your deliberately created beliefs about money and connect with it. The more you do this, the more you will train your mind to think in a new way that will lead to living an abundant and prosperous life.

10

REALITY CHECK

So far we've discussed the fact that:

a) Everything is energy

b) Energy is vibration

c) Our thoughts are energy and vibrations

d) What we think, we send out into the universe

e) Our thoughts have a lot of power

f) We all have a life purpose

g) We all have special gifts and talents

h) Our task in life is to discover those gifts and talents

i) Our thoughts create our reality

j) We need to determine what our goals are

k) We need to focus within and quiet our minds

l) Our thoughts will help us manifest our goals

m) We need to change our belief system

n) We can manifest the life we desire

o) Beliefs are the blueprint of what we will manifest for our lives

Pretty amazing stuff, isn't it? So the summary could read something like this:

If we quiet our minds and look within, we would be able to focus and discover what our true purpose is on this earth. We would be able to use our special gifts and talents, along with a great deal of focus (and discipline) to alter our belief system to create that which we desire for our lives.

WOW!!! Does this mean that if I concentrate really, really hard that George Clooney is going to be standing at my front door with a dozen roses and a ten-carat engagement ring? Or how about I get to fly up in the next space shuttle and help colonize the moon? Or if I start focusing right now and promise to do my visualizations several times a day, I'll get to be the next Queen of England? Maybe if I try hard enough, I'll win the next Powerball Lottery and become a multi-millionaire!

I seriously doubt any of these things are going to manifest themselves in my life – no matter how hard I think about them!

Without a doubt, I believe wholeheartedly in the ability to Manifest the Life you Desire – BUT – I also believe that you must be reasonable in the goals you set yourself. Just as we discussed in the section on goals, you need to assess what brings you joy, what you're good at AND something that you are capable of achieving.

As brilliant as I may be… NASA is not going to come knocking on my door asking me to join the space team unless I'm prepared to put in a LOT of hard work, time, effort and education into achieving my goal of helping to colonize the moon.

And let's face it… Queen Elizabeth is not going to bypass ALL of her relatives to pass her crown to a woman from Texas. That's beyond silly and not a realistic goal at all.

I can't win the lottery, no matter how much I may want to, unless I go out and buy myself a ticket first.

That leaves Mr. Clooney (or any other celebrity) coming to propose to me… Let's get real here… it's not going to happen! Not only am I happily married and well over the age of his preferred companions, I also believe that we are capable of manifesting for ourselves… but not for other people.

Meaning – I believe it's against the Laws of Attraction and the Laws of Nature to interfere with another person's destiny. Call it karma or whatever you'd like – I don't believe in doing that. Same thing with prayer… you can pray for assistance for another, but you should not pray for them to do something that they don't want to do. After all, you certainly wouldn't appreciate it if someone did this for or to you!

Keep these things in mind as we now explore some of the many methods people use to manifest their dreams.

We are now at the point where our journey can be divided into many different directions. One path isn't better than the others – they're all equally effective methods and ways to reach your destination. What matters most is what works and resonates for you AND that you do it regularly. These are the keys to achieving anything you want in your life:

- ~ Look within yourself for what to do
- ~ Respect yourself and others
- ~ Be sincere
- ~ Be consistent
- ~ Be committed
- ~ Don't do anything that might be harmful to another
- ~ Don't let small set-backs stop you
- ~ Be grateful in all things
- ~ Remember that abundance isn't always about money – friends, family, love, health, wisdom, talents, peace - these are all different forms of abundance

If you do these things, any of the following methods will lead you to success:

- ~ Change Your Thoughts – Change Your Life
- ~ Laws of Attraction
- ~ Practicing Affirmations
- ~ Universal Laws
- ~ Attitude of Gratitude
- ~ Vision Boards & Using Your Senses
- ~ Powerful Prayers

11

CHANGE YOUR THOUGHTS – CHANGE YOUR LIFE

We are in the midst of one of the most significant paradigm shifts mankind has ever encountered. We are seeing the a new world that tells us we are interconnected consciousness and that matter is simply another form of energy. Science is quickly catching up with spirituality!

Quantum theory has changed the way we think about everything because what was once viewed as a mechanical, external universe has now become a web of intelligence. Science finally admits that the act of observing changes the result of any experiment, and by extension, that the observer and the observed are not separate.

What follows is a completely new way of dealing with the world as we see it. Now science is telling us that while protons, neutrons and electrons normally behave as waves, when they are observed they act as particles. Observation has the power to change their actions considerably.

That being said, all that we see, hear, taste, touch, smell and feel has been created from the data received by our sensory organs. All we know of the world around us are the mental constructions we assemble from that data. However real and external they may appear, they are phenomena within our minds. This fact is very hard to grasp, as it goes against all of our experience.

If there is anything about which we are certain, it is that the world we are experiencing is real. We can see, touch, feel and hear it. We know it's out there around us, independent and apart from us, existing as a physical world – real, solid and tangible. But according to quantum physics, the world of our experience is no more out there than it is in our dreams.

When we dream, we create our own world, complete with people, places and things that are all separate from us. In the dream everything seems very real, but when we awaken, we realize that everything in the dream was actually a creation of our own mind.

This same process occurs in our waking consciousness. The difference is that now the reality that is created in our world is based on sensory data and bears a closer relationship to what is actually taking place in the real world. No matter how real it may seem, we are not seeing the real world, but an image of that world created in our own mind.

If we consider the reality we experience, then we have to accept that in the final analysis, the physicists are correct:

Consciousness is the essence of everything – everything in the known universe.

So consciousness is the medium from which every aspect of our experience manifests. Every form and quality we ever experience is a construction within consciousness.

What happens when we manifest within the mind?
How is it that consciousness, which is non-material, can take on the material forms that we experience? How do space, time, color, sound, texture, substance, and many other qualities emerge in consciousness?

Whatever we may be conscious of individually, the faculty of consciousness is something that we all share. Consciousness is the one truth we cannot deny and it is the absolute certainty of our existence. It is eternal in that it is always there, regardless of what our experience may be. It is the essence of everything we know and since every aspect of our experience is a manifestation of the mind, it is the creator of the world we know.

The qualities of truth, absoluteness, eternity, essence, and creation among those traditionally associated with God. From this perspective, the statement, "I am God" is not so deluded after all. It might be more accurate to say that, "God is consciousness."

So ultimately what we're saying is that according to science and physics, everything is a manifestation of our mind and we are all connected through consciousness. Bottom line… after thousands of years and billions of dollars… science is now acknowledging that not only is God consciousness… He is all.

12

**LAWS OF ATTRACTION &
PRACTICING AFFIRMATIONS**

The law of attraction states that you attract in your life circumstances and events that are similar or identical to what you focus your thoughts and beliefs on. As we've discussed, every thought has a vibrational energy pattern that will resonate with similar objects and events that already exist or are coming into existence.

Here's an example of how this works: Assume that you hold the belief that taxes are unnecessary and only create financial problems. What happens is that in your life you will attract circumstances that always feel unpleasant when it comes to the topic of taxes. You may find yourself in a conversation where the topic turns to taxes. You'll immediately feel a shift in how you feel. You may get emotional or upset and you'll probably bring up your belief concerning taxes in the conversation.

When tax season comes around, you will become more and more nervous with each passing day, your mind no longer finds rest and ease and even a brief mention of the word *taxes* sucks a huge portion of your attention and energy. In reality, you can experience either positive or negative results. You can either receive a huge return, which would be positive OR your accountant may call and inform you that there are problems and you need to provide additional documents or owe additional money. This would be the negative possibility.

On the other hand, how would this scenario play out if you felt that taxes were a positive way to improve your community and the country? Do you think you would have a more positive experience when tax time came around? With this scenario, you could create an attitude where you make enough money to easily pay your taxes each year and you believe that your accountant is doing a fantastic job of supporting you getting your taxes done in an effortless manner.

What happens is that through the Laws of Attraction, you attract whichever experience you desire. If you want to feel negatively about paying your taxes, you'll have negative experiences. If you have positive feelings and emotions about paying them, you'll attract positive opportunities and situations to you.

You will always attract an outside situation that is matching what's going on inside you, with your belief system and attitude. Your energy will always match with similar energy and you will meet people who are on the same wave length that you are.

You will always attract circumstances in your life that will match what you think and believe.

The question arises – what do you want to attract to your life?

PRACTICING AFFIRMATIONS

Over the years, many teachers have stressed the importance of positive affirmations. These are a wonderful way to help keep you on track! I use them all the time and have always been able to see a difference. BUT – there is one caveat – you need to use the affirmations in a way that will help ingrain them into your being.

Haven't you ever wondered why all these people use affirmations, but nothing seems to change? Often they write them on a sticky note and put them on their computer or bathroom mirror – just waiting for the magic to happen. That's not the way affirmations work.

The best way that I know of to fully integrate affirmations:

YOU have to be actively involved in the process!

None of this work is passive, meaning that you can't just intend on doing it, then wait for the law of attraction to jump in and make you a millionaire.

I have a simple method of working with affirmations, that has been used by thousands of people and it works great!

1. Choose one or two affirmations you want to work with and stick with them for at least one week.

2. Write and say each affirmation aloud at least twice each day. Say it with meaning, with passion, with emphasis.

3. When you are saying the affirmation, actually sense what it feels like. Really feel the affirmation and what it would feel like once it comes to be.

4. When you are writing the affirmation, use a journal or notebook to track the affirmations so you'll see how

consistent you are. Below the affirmation, write out what it means to you. Although you're working with these same affirmations every day for a week, you can still have a different realization or meaning for it each day.

5. Finally, with your journal, write down at least five *different* things that you are grateful for. At first this will be difficult, but once you get started, you'll be amazed at how many wonderful things are already in your life. This will open the door to bringing even more abundance your way.

6. Continue this practice for 45 days, switching-out the affirmations every 5-7 days, taking note of the changes that are being made in your life.

Affirmations to Practice With

Following are some of my favorite affirmations that are guaranteed to be life-changing:

"I am connected to and receiving an unlimited, endless source of abundance!"

"Today I take back my power!"

"I attract and gratefully receive prosperity, abundance and success in my life."

"I receive an unmatchable supply of abundance in my life daily!"

"Opportunities arrive at the right time in the right place."

"I pay my bills with ease because abundance flows freely through me."

"Every day, in every way, I am becoming more prosperous!"

"Miracles manifest every day in wondrous ways."

"My prayers are always answered, in support of my dreams."

"There is limitless supply and it is mine."

"I release all feelings of worry and guilt."

"I am awake to the power I have as an instrument of unconditional love to transform my environment and my life."

"If you see it in your mind, you are going to hold it in your hand."

"I believe in miracles, I believe in fate, I believe that I can make a difference, and I have faith that everything that's happened has made me who I am today."

"In my mind's eye I see health, wealth and wisdom manifesting in my life. I imagine myself going through my day full of energy and vitality."

"Physical reality is a manifestation of thought. You are mentally traveling throughout eternity; now and forever."

"I have unlimited resources of abundance, love and knowledge. I am a wealthy on all levels, physical, mental, emotional, and spiritual."

"All that I desire arises from within me. All life, in fact, arises from within me. Know this, and Awaken."

"Love is mine for the giving. Wealth is mine for the sharing. Wisdom is mine for the waiting."

"I have arrived. I am home in the now. I am solid. I am free. In the ultimate I dwell. What a loving place to be."

"I now release anger in positive ways. I love and appreciate myself. I only speak words that are loving and constructive."

"Limitations live only in our minds. But if we use our imaginations, our possibilities become limitless."

"I am visible, I matter, I am heard, I am me, My inner-fire revitalizes me, The more I move the more I am energized, I have the courage to release my fiery passion for my highest good and the highest good of all!"

"I have the wisdom to bring my dreams and aspiration to fruition. Each day my dreams become clearer to me."

"It is indeed a wondrous day that is filled with endless possibilities. I enjoy the magnificence of who I am!"

I am declaring to myself that my long journey of awakening is complete. I am a fully awakened Being. I know who I am. I AM that I AM. And I declare: "I AM the revealing Presence of Divine Love in Action".

"You are Blessed - this is the message you have been waiting for!"

"Limitations live only in our minds. But if we use our imaginations, our possibilities become limitless."

"It is in loving and serving others that we find our true Self and tap into the Loving Abundance of the Universe."

"The longer I live, the more beautiful life becomes."

"Today a new sun rises for me; everything lives, everything is animated, everything seems to speak to me of my passion, everything invites me to cherish it."

"You are the designer of your destiny. You are the author. You write the story. The pen is in your hand, and the outcome is whatever you choose."

"I am a magnificent child of God, able to do great things as my Father has taught me. I am beautiful, I am strong, I am capable of providing whatever is needed. I am Blessed!"

13

UNIVERSAL LAWS

With the plethora of books being written on the laws of attraction, there are many, many Universal Laws being discussed. As with everything, some of these will resonate with you, while others might not. What is important is that you keep an open mind and continue exploring and learning.

These spiritual laws are provided to you to allow you to have a different perspective on issues that may come up in your life and assist you getting through it. They may help you have an "aha!" moment, so that you can effect changes quickly. Once you have a sudden shift in perspective, everything can change for the better very quickly.

1. **You have a hidden source of power.** In our day-to-day living, we often become tired, discouraged, anxious or even overwhelmed. This is a prime time to tap into your hidden source of power to become recharged and ready to go again. What is this source? Joy! Don't ever let anyone steal your joy!

   When things seem to be getting you down, just think back to a time in your life, to a special memory of a moment when you experienced overwhelming joy and peace. Relive this moment in your mind and you'll begin to start feeling better, more relaxed and ready to face whatever comes your way. This sounds very simple… but can be extremely powerful when practiced. Go to your 'happy place' and you'll begin to feel the difference immediately - it's another wonderful gift from your mind and consciousness to help you cope in times of stress and it works!

2. **We all make deadly vows.** That sounds pretty awful – and it sometimes can be. Most people don't realize it at the time, but in times of stress or great need, they have often made a deal with God, the Universe, or whomever. "If I can just get past/survive _____, I'll do anything!" or "Please give me _____ and I'll never ask for anything again!" or something similar. We've all said and done this a time or two.

   A deadly vow is a bargain or a deal sacrificing something to get something else in exchange. Most of the time it pertains to money, but it can be most anything. Quite often, we agree to sacrifice love or relationships. When that happens, we start looking for substitutes to replace the missing 'love'. We form addictions in order to avoid the pain to the point where we are missing out on life.

I made one of these vows myself many years ago. My 12-year old daughter had a serious infection that we didn't know about and ended-up having a grand mal seizure at school. When we were notified and rushed to the hospital, she was unresponsive and still thrashing from the seizure that she'd had over an hour before.

We eventually had to put her in a medically induced coma for several days for testing and to help her brain and body heal from this traumatic event. Since she was my only child – and a miracle baby at that – I was making all sorts of deals with God for her to wake-up unharmed and healthy.

In my 'deadly vow' I asked God to give me the problem, to take it from my daughter and give it to me, so that she could be healthy and strong again. Several days later, by the grace of God, we discovered the virus that she had contracted, began treating it and reduced her medication so that she could begin waking-up from her coma. It took a few days for her to fully recover, but she had no damage, no problems, no residual complications for this severe and traumatic event. On the other hand, a few weeks later, I was hospitalized with the deadly staph infection, MRSA.

Because of the damage that the MRSA had done on my body – thanks to my vow – it destroyed my immune system, creating the perfect situation for me to develop Chronic Fatigue Syndrome, Epstein Barr, and Common Variable Immunodeficiency. All meaning that I was exhausted, had about 20 horrible symptoms and side-effects and my body no longer created immunoglobulin, so I couldn't fight-off any diseases.

Fortunately, after a few years of suffering with these diseases and taking 1,000's of pills and infusions, I began working with an energy healer – ultimately learning how to heal myself and am now completely symptom-free and perfectly healthy. Trust me… you don't want to experience something like this on your own. While I don't regret my 'bargain' with God to save my daughter's life – I've since learned that it's not really necessary to make these deals or vows. Prayer, faith and belief in His ability to heal is quite enough all on its own. Know and believe that He has a Divine Plan and that he'll take care of everything – with or without your vows.

How do we break the vow once we've made it and get past this? Look for past trauma in your life. Look for when the substitute or addictive behaviors began. You can break the vow when you stop the substitute behavior and heal the original memory of what occurred when the vow was taken. Use that beautiful mind of yours to create a new memory – one that doesn't require bargains or making deals. Make peace with yourself and your circumstances and you'll begin to heal this destructive behavior and start to soar!

3. **Negative programming will ruin your day!** Everyone one of us wakes up with the potential to have a great day. But… that doesn't always happen. Sometimes we are already negatively programmed because we know what the day is going to bring and we're dreading it. Others end-up manifesting a bad day by creating their own negative programming.

There are two things that will immediately get your day off to a bad start… expectation and comparison.

One of the key components of living a more positive life is getting rid of expectation. Stop focusing on the end result as this will take you away from what you want instead of toward it. It's great to focus on what you want… but not obsessing or worrying about it. Set your goals, make your plan, then get on with living in the moment. If you fixate only on the end result, you'll become anxious, worried and probably disappointed.

Comparison should really be considered one of the seven deadly sins. It comes from judging yourself and others. Comparison puts you in the 'why me' mode or jealousy, neither of which are productive nor will help you live a more productive and positive life. As we discussed earlier, we all create our circumstances and if you are constantly judging and comparing your situation with others, you'll never have the time or energy to manifest the life you desire.

Comparison will put you in one of two places… neither of which are good. You'll either start feeling superior/egotistical or inferior/less worthy. If you focus on your goals, gifts and talents, you won't have time for these negative feelings and emotions, and you'll be on the road to manifesting a terrific life for yourself.

4. **Your beliefs determine everything you think, feel and do.** Everything we do is because of something we believe. Understanding your beliefs can help you get a handle on why you do what you do, why you're thinking what you think, why you're doing what you do. You have to learn to understand

your beliefs if you want to change your behavior and therefore your life.

According to Dr. Bruce Lipton, 98% of our wrong beliefs come from programming that occurs before the age of six years old. In those first six years, we don't have the logic or reasoning to say, "That doesn't make any sense to me" or "I'm not going to feel that way". We don't have the ability to judge and evaluate the circumstances that happen to us and are programmed to believe that what happens to us is normal, no matter how painful, pleasurable, wonderful or terrible. This is why so many adults have problems stemming from their childhood – their parents or other adults programmed them one way, then after they became older, they formed their own beliefs which may be contradictory to what they were originally told.

To lead your ideal life, you have to change the negative beliefs that programmed you to live the way you are now. You'll need to address both the conscious and unconscious beliefs you have been living with. To truly live the life you want to manifest, you will need to correct the negative programming and then you'll see your problems fall away and your life can take off in a way you've never imagined by using willpower and effort.

5. **When in doubt – look within.** This one is so simple... when you have questions or need to make decisions and don't know what to do... just look within. We all have many decisions to make on a daily basis, and sometimes we don't know what the correct answer is. When in doubt – look within. A dear friend says that we need to be peaceful enough so we can hear that little angel on our shoulder tell us the right thing to do. This is so true – listen and look within!!

Your conscience is connected to the universal energy consciousness and when we are quiet and still, we'll receive the answers we need. When you must make a difficult decision, test your answers. Feel if a particular answer is causing you distress in any way. If it does... it's not the right one! If the answer makes you feel at peace, then that's the way to go. It sounds simple, but many times the right answer isn't always the popular or obvious one. That's when you really need to take the 'peace test' to determine how you really feel with each answer.

Keep in mind that 99% of your wisdom is in your heart... not your brain! When you try to think logically every time, there's a good chance that you'll be missing something. So remember, when making difficult decisions, ask yourself this question when thinking about answers, "Do I have peace when I choose this or does my peace go away?"

6. **You can create joy and peace now.** Everyone wants to be happy. Everyone deserves to be happy. Everyone CAN be happy. Sounds simple, but is it really possible? Yes! Generally, there are two things that block joy and peace in almost every situation. Either the person is focusing too much on the past or they are focusing too much one the future in a negative way. We dwell on negative things that have happened to us in the past and we anticipate negative things happening to us in the future.

The fact is that 90% of the negative things we anticipate for the future don't actually happen the way we were anticipating. Yet... because our minds create our reality, we can believe or create the negative behavior and live it before it happens to us. Honestly, why would any of us want to do this to ourselves?

It's more difficult dealing with past issues, but here's a quick way to begin releasing them. Write down two or three things from the past that bring up negative emotions for you. Besides those items, write, "Yet I survived!" then add "I'm going to now heal those places within me and live my life to the fullest!". If you start thinking about things that happened to you in the past, just remind yourself that you survived and be grateful for what you learned through the experience.

Now write down two or three things that you are anticipating will be negative in the future. Next to those items, write three ways in which you can change these from a negative to a positive and focus on that. Every time your mind wanders to these potential negative situations, mentally transform them into positive experiences and how you can make them work out for the best for everyone.

This is part of manifesting the life you desire... turning potential negatives into positives!

7. **You ARE NOT the problem, you only *have* the problem.** Typically people believe that they are the problem. They so closely identify with the problem that they take ownership and consider it part of themselves. That is NOT true!

Many people believe that if they have a problem, then something is wrong with them or that they're not worth as much as others. Nothing could be further from the truth!

We are all basically wonderful and good human beings - some have problems that may change their outlook on the world, but that doesn't change the spirit/soul that their body carries. It's the same with those who are severely disabled. Their bodies may be damaged, but their spirit/soul is still pure.

It's like getting a splinter. The splinter is in your finger and it might hurt. You can see and feel it. You can have negative thoughts and emotions about it… but YOU are not the splinter. It's just a piece of wood that's inside your skin that needs to be removed. It doesn't change who you are… it just needs to come out. When it does, you'll heal and be just fine. Think of your problems being the same as that splinter. Work them out and you'll return to a more pure self.

I have a wonderful friend who has had epilepsy her entire life, but she never allowed the potential of seizures to slow her down one bit. She's been married to the same man for over 30 years, has a beautiful daughter who's recently got married, has a job she loves and a very active social life. Seizures? Who needs them! She takes care of herself, but she never allowed the disease to define her.

Dr. Bruce Lipton, from the Stanford Medical School, says that the beliefs we hold in our unconscious and subconscious minds are more than a million times more powerful than our willpower. That's why it's so hard to change these problems with willpower alone. You'll need to really put an effort into this, keep it in perspective and make conscious and focused changes in your life.

Identify yourself with who you really are:

a wonderful, fabulous, perfect, valuable,

pure Being who is capable of

manifesting the life that you desire.

14

ATTITUDE OF GRATITUDE

"Finding the joy in every day" this is one of my favorite ways of manifesting. The belief is simple, be grateful for all you've been given. Say thank you each and every day. What could possibly be easier?

As a child most of us are taught that we should say "Please" and "Thank You", but somehow these things start slipping our minds once we become older. Ironically, they slip our minds more often when we are dealing with God – when we should be applying them the most!

When you think about it, when we do something for someone and we're thanked and know that the person appreciates it, we're more likely to do something for them again next time. Why wouldn't God be the same way? He isn't that much different from us in some ways and I believe He still likes to be thanked for the Blessings He sends us.

Keeping a Gratitude Journal is a wonderful way of not only remembering to say thank you, it's also an amazing record of all the Blessings in our lives. Whenever you're down… just go through that journal and it'll brighten your day immediately! You don't have to create an exhaustive list every day, just one or two things.

If journaling isn't your thing… jot down a couple items on your daily calendar. Keep in mind that Blessings aren't necessarily huge things like world peace or curing cancer. Sometimes a Blessing is something as simple as finding a flower blooming or receiving a smile from a stranger walking down the street. Blessings come in all sizes, shapes and descriptions. Sometimes, they're even a little 'back-handed'.

There was a time when I wanted a basketball goal taken down from our new home, but my husband was reluctant to remove it. One day, a huge wind storm came up and we had very powerful gusts blowing. All of a sudden I heard a crash and discovered that the wind had very neatly blown the basketball goal down, pole and all. It had broken off cleanly and it never blocked my view of hills and pastures again!

Listing your Blessings is a great way to stay positive and focused. No matter who you are or what your circumstances happen to be – you have received at least one Blessing each and every day. Remember it, appreciate it, thank God for it. You'll be surprised how the Blessings will begin growing, like a snowball rolling down the hill, getting bigger and coming faster by the moment. Soon you'll be overwhelmed by Blessings!

Of course, the other side of this is that you need to begin giving and sending out Blessings to others. Since Blessings don't have to cost anything… you should be doing this all the time. Share a smile, hold the door open for someone, give a homeless person a dollar, hug someone - keep in mind that these don't have to be grand gestures.

Oftentimes the smallest, kindest gestures are the ones that are most needed or valued.

Giving Blessings can be just as rewarding as receiving them, as Blessings can make the world a happier place. Giving Blessings should be done without the expectation of a return, it is not a transaction. A Blessing is a gift given freely to others yet can enhance and expand our lives, as well. A Blessing sets us free, not to be irresponsible, but to become more of who we are or who we are capable of being.

So what exactly is a Blessing, you might ask. They generally come with three criteria:

- ~ First, a Blessing enhances the life of a person or other living creature or enhances the functionality of an object. Because of the Blessing they have more of that they need to fulfill their potential.

- ~ Second, a Blessing is unobstructing in some way. It opens up a space in which we can see and move in new directions. It gives us an experience of the unobstructed world, it makes us less constricted.

- ~ Third, a Blessing connects us in a deeper way with our world, allowing us to feel a greater sense of belonging and wholeness. It connects us with the circulation of the blood and breath of spirit amongst us all.

A Blessing is not a technique we perform, but a presence we embody. It's a relationship we form that enables us to embrace them and their spirit with our own.

Since everyone is unique, each of us will have our own way of Blessing others. There is no right or wrong way to do this. It is the intent and spirit of the act that actually gives the Blessing.

We are all worthy and capable of giving and receiving Blessings. This is not a special power or skill reserved for the spiritually elite, but something that is inherent in each of us as a natural expression. Think about a parent comforting a child… that's a Blessing.

A Blessing isn't something you 'do' to someone, but it's something that you give to them. It can be a kind word, a hug, a glance, a ritual, just listening, playing music, anything at all. It can be a special mantra, a ceremony or laying on of hands. Blessings are not reserved for the 'holy' or 'pious', but for anyone or anything. Yes, I believe animals can give Blessings, as I have been the recipient of those, as well.

The most beautiful and poignant Blessing I ever received was given to me by my horse on the day he died. I have never felt so much love being given to me as I did on that day by him. It was an overwhelmingly beautiful experience and something that I will always cherish. Animals have souls, too, and should never be discounted.

Remember, if you can love, you can Bless. It's really that simple and it's one of the best ways to honor others, yourself and God. When you're creating the list of goals you'd like to manifest, don't forget to include being grateful and sending out Blessings to others. It will improve the quality of your life in ways infinitely more valuable than material possessions ever could.

15

VISION BOARDS & USING YOUR SENSES

Vision boards are a great way to help manifest what it is you want for your life, in fact it's the best way I've come across for those of us who are more visually inclined.

The concept is simple, create a bulletin board of all the things you'd like to manifest in your life: a relationship, a child, a new home, new vehicles, a new job, large checking account, vacations, that new sailboat… whatever it is you'd like to manifest for yourself and your family. When you have these reminders facing you every day, it'll help you stay focused and on track.

What type of vision board do you want to create? You can use one of the little inexpensive fabric and ribbon covered boards that you find in hobby stores, use a magnetic dry-erase board so that you can write affirmations on, in addition to adding photos, or simply a sheet of posterboard that you hang-up in your bedroom, kitchen, office... wherever you will see it the most.

Remember that this is your board, so put anything up on it that you want to manifest. Find photos in magazines, on the internet, in books, whatever you can find that will express what it is you want to manifest for your life – this is all about YOU and what you want for your life. Get creative! Go find some fabulous photos of the exact lifestyle you'd like to have and put them on your board.

Another thing that people like to put on their vision boards is Abundance Checks. These are wonderful because you can make them out for whatever you want. Write in what you're asking the Universe for, a date for receipt and go for it! Put several of these up on your vision board to remind yourself of what it is you're manifesting. We've provided you with a blank abundance check to copy and fill-out over and over again. We like to write new ones during the New Moon. That's a wonderful time to start projects, because the moon and Earth's energies are working with you.

While you're writing-out your check, feel what it would be like to actually have whatever it is you want, right there in your hands. If your check is for $20,000 what would it be like to actually have a check in your hands for that amount of money. Really feel it! What would you do with that amount of money? Would you feel relief because you could pay some bills? Would you be excited to go on that trip you've always wanted? See that money in your checking account. Really get into it!

KNOW that this money is yours – claim it! Feel it down to your bones and know that the Universe will provide it to you.

Maybe you want a new sports car. Think about how wonderful it would be driving that new car. Feel the keys in your hand. What does it smell like? How fast does it go? Feel yourself sliding into those soft leather seats, shifting gears and listening to that amazing stereo system. Feel the wind in your hair as you cruise in your new car up and down country roads, enjoying the sheer power of that new sports car.

Manifesting The Life You Desire

Bank of the Unlimited Universe
Where we manifest your desires!

PAY: _____

TO THE ORDER OF: _____

Unlimited Universe ॐ
Unlimited Abundance Account

DATE: _____

$ _____

Non Negotiable
YOU MUST BELIEVE TO RECEIVE

SIGNED: _____

Pilongton Healing Light

www.healinglightonline.com

⑈123 45678⑈ 11:11:11

The more senses you employ, the more powerful the visualization becomes to you and the closer you are to manifesting what it is you're looking for.

The same thing goes for all the items on your vision board, sense them, feel them, *know* that these things are coming to you! The more you put into your visualizations, the more powerful your manifestations will become.

Get specific! Tell the God and the Universe exactly what you want. Don't just say that you want a job. Ask for and expect the perfect job:

- ~ Ask for the field of work that you're most interested in.
- ~ Ask for the best location for your job and commute.
- ~ Ask for the right salary… what do you want to make at this perfect job?
- ~ Ask for the right boss, someone who understands your situation or preferences.
- ~ Ask for the right work schedule… those days and hours that best suit your schedule. If you want to go to school while working, put that in your request so that your new job won't

prevent you from achieving what you want.

By asking for these very specific things, you aren't requesting yourself out of a job – you're letting God and the Universe exactly what you want and need. If you don't... you're liable to come up with any "old thing" that you won't be happy with in the long run.

Get yourself a spiral notebook and spend time writing each day about what you want to manifest. Again – get specific about what you are asking for. The Universe won't provide you with the "perfect situation" until you let them know exactly what you want.

You can write about what you're going to do with the $20,000 you're asking for or simply write, "$20,000 is coming to me this month from the Universe. This is my Divine Right – this money is mine and I claim it today!"

They may not happen today, or tomorrow, or by the end of next week, BUT... if you really believe, feel, sense, and know that this is coming to you... guess what? It will!

This not only happens for me, but it happens for others that I know, as well. This has worked with jobs, homes, vehicles, relationships... you name it! Just remember that you need to involve as many of your senses as possible when working with a specific 'request' from the Universe.

Remember that this doesn't have to always be about material things. It can be for other situations – there's no such thing as bizarre to the Universe. When preparing to have my daughter, I was considered a bit of a risk and terrified of labor. I wrote pages in my notebook, saying, "I am having an effortless, quick, and pain-free labor and delivery."

So how was it? It was natural and lasted four hours from the first pain until I held my daughter in my arms. How's that for a great manifestation?

Remember that the sky's the limit… as long as you aren't trying to create something for someone else or forcing someone else to do what you want. Manifesting is about creating for YOU!

Whether you decide to create a vision board, journal, write-out abundance checks, visualize or use everything together (what I recommend), make certain that you do it daily. Rome wasn't built in a day and neither will your empire. The Universe will provide – but you have to put in an effort, too.

Manifesting is really fun! The more you do it, the better you'll become. You can start-off with small things and build-up to that huge mansion on the hill.

You can't go into this 'half-way'...
you MUST Believe to Receive!

16

POWERFUL PRAYERS

Prayer is one of the key components in manifesting the life you desire, along with determining your goals, finding your special gifts and talents, discovering your belief systems and creating your new, more positive reality.

Some might ask, "What really is prayer?"

- ~ Prayer is a way of channeling and transmitting energy. It can bring joy, inspiration, healing, peace, exhilaration – and even bliss.

- It is not an obligation or a meaningless chore, but a vibrant, living power.
- It is not the deluded hope of someone crying out in desperation, but the practical solution to a myriad of problems.
- It is not an act of fear or false piety, but one of courage and true love.

If prayer were understood and practiced every day by more people, not only would those people's lives change, but the whole world would change. After all, prayer works!

We've all prayed for things, from getting a puppy or making an A on a test in grade school, to getting the right date for the prom, to finding that perfect job, healing someone dear, or helping us meet that special someone to share the rest of our lives with. I believe that everyone on this earth has prayed at least once or twice. All of us have done it to ask for something that we really, really wanted.

But what is *real* prayer? Now that's something a little different from is normally done or even taught. Real prayer is selfless and is invoked through the power of love. As the great yogi Swami Vivekananda once stated, "The moment you have succeeded in manufacturing love out of prana (energy), you are free." The prayer must be conditioned out of love and we must send out a lot of loving energy in the process.

Of course, regardless of how fervently we may pray, some prayers just don't seem to be answered the way we'd like. That goes back to the Eastern philosophy of karma. It might just be that the situation or circumstances aren't supposed to unfold the way you've been praying. Sometimes God has a greater plan that you just aren't able to change or influence. When viewed in this light, there isn't any need to feel doubt because a prayer wasn't answered the way you wanted. I once heard a phrase that I absolutely love about prayer,

"Sometimes rejection is God's way of protection!"

We don't always see the ramifications of what we're asking for and sometimes it's best if we don't receive it. There's a song that goes, "One of God's greatest gifts is unanswered prayer." He always knows what's best for us, where we usually are a little short-sighted on the subject.

Prayer is a natural power – not a superstition. With the right quality and quantity of spiritual energy, anything can be accomplished and the world can be transformed.

We can all help to improve the world and our own lives by becoming a channel of the unlimited energy of love, in thought, word, deed or prayer. You'll be amazed at the transformation when you try it!

Prayer is an expression of energy, in addition to love. Real love is not a measure of emotion, but something much greater. Being able to channel the extraordinary power of love brings freedom from hate and a host of other things. Love can bring freedom from war, disease, and our own basic selves. Instead of thinking of love as an emotion or a state of mind, consider it as a state of being. You don't have to love each and every person you meet, but you can love them in an impersonal sense in that you desire the highest good for them. When God told us to love our enemies, he didn't mean have them over for dinner, but to love and respect their spirit/soul. That way, we abolish hate, just as water extinguishes fire. So, in a sense, our prayers can become the fountain from which the water of love flows.

This love can heal, transform, change ourselves and the world. It may sound like a fairy tale, but we have the potential to make this happen and have seen it happen in our lifetime. Look at the things Mother Teresa did, sharing love all over India and transforming lives. In the present day we have Amma, nicknamed the Hugging Saint. This woman spends each day hugging thousands of people. They travel hundreds of miles and stand in line for hours just to receive a hug from this woman. Why? Because she shares pure unadulterated love with each person she sees. There is nothing like Amma's hugs… they are truly magical and her blessings are incredibly strong. What you ask for, you will receive, she is that strong in faith.

There is something to love, prayers, energy, vibrations, frequencies, manifesting - it's all here and it's all very real. We may not be able to see it, but it can be felt by everyone and it can affect our lives, health, relationships and well-being.

Yes, Thoughts Are Energy

As we've said many times, thoughts are energy, so everything we think affects the world around us, as well as our own lives. You brain is an amazing instrument that allows you to not only send out this energy, but receive it as well. You can almost 'tune-in' to frequencies, whether they be the basic and Earthly or the esoteric and inspirational. Isn't it wonderful that you can decide which channels you want to concentrate on?

When people wallow in negative thoughts, bitterness, anger, resentment, jealousy and other negative emotions, they are not only harming themselves, but everyone around them. They keep themselves in a very low form of mindset and by sending out this harmful energy, they are bringing others down to their level. Then they wonder why their circumstances are always so unhappy and lash out at others. They've brought it all on themselves, but generally refuse to accept responsibility for their negativity and actions, assigning blame on everything and everyone around them. These people have become toxic to themselves and everyone around them.

The concept of positive thinking has been around for quite a while now and has been proven effective time and time again. Positive praying is like putting this concept into overdrive – what incredible results you can have! Not only will your life and circumstances improve, but you'll lift-up others and help make the world a better place. Being filled with positive thoughts, feelings, gratitude, kindness, compassion, a love of life and selflessness enhances your life, your health, relationships – every aspect of your life. When your brain is attuned to these higher frequencies/vibrations, you become a channel for spiritual energy and can achieve great things for yourself and others.

It's not always easy to stay positive, perky and happy. Things can and do get us down, old habits die hard and that monkey mind can break loose and go crazy at times. When this happens, we have to want to work to make a change in our lives for the better. We have to *choose* to make the effort to be positive.

Quantum theory has proven to us that

life doesn't just happen to us...

we have the ability to make the changes we desire!

When we get stuck sometimes it's good to use affirmations. These can have a tremendous effect on the brain and the emotions. Even saying, "Every day in every way I am getting better and better" can have a very positive effect on your mindset. Of course, you need to say affirmations that are true and even if you don't completely believe it at the moment – fake it until you make it!

The ultimate way to raise our energy/frequency/vibration level is in prayer.

Communion with God is the most elevating experience you can have. Once you become good at prayer, you will become more and more positive in your daily life. The more positive you are, the better your praying will become and the more positive you will be. The more positive you are, the better reality you'll be able to manifest for yourself. It's like a beautiful, antique hand-carved merry-go-round – all you have to do is jump on and enjoy the relaxing ride.

The secret to manifesting the life you desire is not a secret at all.

It is the conscious effort and decision on your part to:

- ~ Discovering your purpose, special gifts and talents
- ~ Defining the goals you want to achieve
- ~ Determining your path
- ~ Focusing on your thoughts
- ~ Creating your new, positive mind-set
- ~ Sending out gratitude and blessings
- ~ Praying with a Purpose

17

PUTTING IT ALL TOGETHER

We've talked about a lot of different techniques for manifestation, so what do we do next? Once you read something like this, it's easy to understand and believe, but sometimes it's more difficult to actually sit down and start putting it into practice in your daily life.

Once you've completed the earlier exercises, discovering exactly who you are and what you want to accomplish for your life, it's time to put those thoughts, dreams and ideas into action. Here are 10 Steps to help you achieve your goals and put you on the fast track to manifesting.

Step 1

What is it that really makes you happy?

_____

_____

_____

Step 2

Discover your purpose:

What is your deepest desire? _____

_____

_____

What would you like to accomplish in your life? _____

_____

_____

What are you good at? _____

_____

_____

What makes you feel complete? _____

_____

_____

What resonates within you? _____

_____

_____

Is there something you feel particularly drawn to? _____

_____

Step 3

Find what you do best:

What would you do if you never had to work again?_____

_____

What were your dreams when you were younger? _____

_____

What do you think is impossible for you to do? _____

_____

What would you do if this were the last day of your life? _____

_____

What would you do if you knew you only had one year to live? _____

_____

_____

What would you do if you knew you couldn't fail? _____

_____

_____

What are your strengths and talents? _____

_____

_____

Do you have a wish but don't know how to fulfill it? _____

_____

_____

What do you admire most about others? _____

_____

_____

What would your idea lifestyle look like? _____

_____

_____

_____

What does success mean to you? _____

_____

_____

_____

What really makes you happy? _____

_____

_____

What would be a perfect day for you? _____

_____

_____

What would you do if there were no restrictions? _____

_____

_____

What really excites you? _____

_____

_____

_____

What would you like to be honored and recognized for? _____

_____

_____

Where do you see your life in ten years? _____

_____

_____

_____

If you were immortal, what would you do with your life? _____

_____

_____

What needs to change to make this a better world? _____

_____

_____

What would you do if you could do anything? _____

What are you most proud of? _____

What would you like to accomplish this year? _____

What would you do differently if you could start over again? _____

Given the time, money and opportunity – what would you most like to accomplish? _____

_____

_____

_____

Step 4

Re-Discover who you are:

What are your special gifts and talents? _____

_____

_____

_____

How can you use them to change your life? _____

_____

_____

What steps can you take today to start making those changes? _____

_____

_____

Step 5
Focus on your potential and use your imagination:

What is that you want to manifest? _____

_____

_____

Describe what it feels like to achieve this goal: _____

_____

_____

_____

_____

How will this look? _____

_____

_____

How will your life change once you achieve this goal? _____

_____

_____

_____

Describe how you see this accomplishment: _____

_____

_____

_____

_____

Step 6

Now that you know what your goal is, it's time to write your affirmations. Write a new one to use each week, for 6 weeks.

I AM now manifesting _____

_____

this or something better, for the highest and greatest good of all.

I AM now manifesting _____

_____

this or something better, for the highest and greatest good of all.

I AM now manifesting _____

_____

this or something better, for the highest and greatest good of all.

I AM now manifesting _____

_____

this or something better, for the highest and greatest good of all.

I AM now manifesting _____

_____

this or something better, for the highest and greatest good of all.

I AM now manifesting _____

_____

this or something better, for the highest and greatest good of all.

Step 7

Brain check – are you keeping positive thoughts flowing?

Let's add some more loving, positive, re-affirming statements to fill your mind when those negative thoughts threaten to creep in:

"I am well on my way to achieving _____

_____."

"The Universe is supporting me in manifesting _____

_____."

"Every day, in every way I am getting stronger and achieving more towards my goal of _____

_____."

Add some of your own below:

_____

_____

_____

_____

Step 8

Create your vision board, using photos, phrases, abundance checks, whatever you can think of to have a visual representation of what you want to achieve.

Step 9

Being grateful and getting your senses involved. Start writing your affirmations in a notebook. Once you've written the affirmation, write a brief sentence about what it means to you. This will be something different every time you do it.

Along with your daily affirmation, list at least five things you're grateful for each day. Make certain that this list is different each day... dig down deep to appreciate even the smallest of things in your life. By doing this, you'll open the doors for more and larger blessings to come in.

Step 10

Honest and sincere prayer. There can't be enough said about an honest prayer asking for guidance and assistance from above. Once you've taken a few minutes to write your affirmations and gratitude list, say a short prayer asking for Divine Guidance and assistance in achieving your goals. A little prayer can go a long ways!

"All that we are is the result of what we have thought; it is founded on our thoughts, it is made up of our thoughts.

If a man speaks or acts with a pure thought, happiness follows him, like a shadow that never leaves him." ~ Buddha

ABOUT THE AUTHOR

Teri Van Horn is dedicated to healing the body, mind and spirit through holistic and spiritual means.

She provides Reiki treatments, crystal healing and intuitive readings to heal the physical body, in addition to providing Life Coaching, with a spiritual focus to assist you in creating the life you desire. Her goal is to assist others in reaching their highest potential.

Teri has been a student of Spirituality for over 30 years, studying ancient religions, world religion and New Age principals. She has attended sessions with Linda Howe, Carmen Butler, Betty Eadie, Doreen Virtue, Wayne Dyer, Alberto Villoldo, Steve Jones, and others, although she states that Edgar Cayce was her earliest and most influential 'teacher'. Teri has benefited by studying with world renowned healers, in addition to being a 5th generation Karuna and Usui/Tibetan Reiki Master.

She has become a powerful intuitive healer and excels in working with Distant, Shamanic, and Crystal Healing, as well as Psychic Protection and Clearing. Teri's healing specialties include opening, clearing and working with the chakras, and psychic protection, in addition to healing physical ailments and diseases.

Teri also has a very special connection with animals and has been treating them with Reiki for many years. Specializing in horses and companion animals, she has been able to make dramatic changes in them physically and emotionally. There are no bad animals... only those who have experienced traumatic events and Teri has been able to heal many problems with pets thru the use of Distant Healing. Additionally, she works in conjunction with veterinarians to help speed the recovery of animals who are sick or injured.

Teri has an extensive knowledge-base of crystals and works with them to heal the body, mind and spirit. She is a sought-after lecturer regarding crystals and how they work for us and holds seminars teaching others how to use and work with their energies.

We are all energy beings... therefore, our thoughts and feelings (conscious and subconscious) are constantly influencing our physical realities. Teri explains, "I help people discover what is most needed in this moment now, in order to fully envision how the best possible reality looks and feels. I bring many years of training and experience in spirituality and business, together with natural intuition to provide people with the necessary inspiration, direction, and support to create their best possible lives."

Teri and her husband, William, live on a small ranch in Texas with their nine horses, four dogs and three doves. She spends her free time working with the animals and her herb garden.

Teri provides healing sessions both in person and through distant healing, in addition to intuitive readings. She teaches workshops on Reiki, working with crystals, psychic protection and manifesting.

You can reach Teri thru her website at
www.healinglightonline.com

Made in the USA
Columbia, SC
21 September 2018